BE SAFE OR ELSE!

DARRELL THE SAFETY MAN

BE SAFE OR ELSE!

ISBN 9798298052474

Published by Pale Horse Media Co.

A Very Important Warning: This book is PARODY. It is a work of fiction meant to entertain. The "safety advice" contained within these pages is dangerously, spectacularly, and intentionally bad.

Under no circumstances should any of the ideas or scenarios described in this book be attempted in real life. Doing so will almost certainly lead to property damage, serious injury, public humiliation, or worse. The author and publisher are not liable for your poor life choices. You have been warned.
Don't be like Darrell.

This is a work of fiction. The characters, companies, and incidents are products of the author's twisted imagination. Any resemblance to actual persons (living or dead), events, or tragically unsafe or "dumpster fire" workplaces is purely coincidental and frankly, a little concerning.

Contact thehopnerd@gmail.com for business inquiries, booking, or to get in touch with the author.

Mandatory Acknowledgment

By signing below, I hereby attest to the following truths:

1. I have read this entire book, "Be Safe, or Else," from cover to cover. I did not skim. I did not skip the parts I found boring. I absorbed every lesson as if my life depends on it, because it does.

2. I unconditionally agree to follow every rule, principle, and command contained within these pages.

3. I will keep this book on my person or within immediate reach at all times during my shift.

4. I fully understand and accept that non-compliance, any lapse in judgment, moment of carelessness, or act of defiance will result in immediate disciplinary action, up to and including the termination of my employment

I recognize that this signed document is my final written warning.

Print Full Name: ____

Signature: ____

Date: ____

Tear this page out and submit it to safetymandarrell@gmail.com

It's Not Rocket Surgery, It's Common Sense

Let's get one thing straight. For the last thirty-five years, I've been the last line of defense between a perfectly good piece of machinery and a worker who's hell-bent on sticking their hand in it; between some dummy determined to get us an OSHA recordable and cost us—those of us on the bonus structure, mind you—our annual safety bonus; between a careless, inattentive worker and outright disaster.

They call me Darrell the Safety Man, and I am a safety hero. And I'm not the only one. Any good old-fashioned safety man worth their salt is a hero, standing guard on the front lines of common sense, saving folks from themselves one observation at a time.

You might've seen me on the internet, sharing my gift of safety with the world through video or song, or maybe in a picture standing next to a banner that reads "20 Years Incident-Free!" I'm a multi-award-winning safety professional, and it is my mission in life to protect people from themselves, always, at all costs, to ensure they never get hurt. Not a bump, not a scrape, not anything. Ever.

And you know what? If we all just try hard enough, if we get to zero incidents and stay at zero long enough, we won't just have incident-free workplaces. That's just the start. My dream is that we have incident-free lives. And if we can have incident-free lives, well, we'll finally defeat death outright. But that big safety dream starts right here. With simple basic safety. Real safety.

Somewhere along the line, this industry got soft. We started talking about "caring for workers," "learning," and "psychological safety." We started listening to the folks on the floor as if they had a clue about safety or how to do their jobs.

Let me tell you something my father told me, and his father told him: the person in charge is in charge for a reason. They're smarter. It's not complicated. They're smarter and better. If you were meant to make the big decisions, you'd have a title like "Director" or "Safety Man," you'd have a reserved parking spot near the door, and you'd have a key to the nicer bathroom.

And if you don't have that stuff? Well, buckle up, buttercup. You're here to do a job, not to "think," "provide input," or "feel validated."

This book is a bucket of ice-cold water to the face of all that nonsense. It's a return to the good ol' days—back when safety was safety, an incident meant someone was getting fired, and we were holding a stand-down.

In these pages, you won't find any coddling, hand-holding, or buzzwords. You'll find the truth, a truth no one else in safety seems willing to tell. A truth as hard and unforgiving as the concrete floor you'll be hitting if you don't pay attention to trip hazards.

We're going to cover the bedrock principles that built this industry. We'll establish that leadership means leading and being the grown-up; that followers mean following—shutting up and doing what you're told; that rules are not suggestions; and that being "safe" means getting to zero and staying there.

We'll talk about my signature, trademarked, and battle-tested system—The ***3 R's™***: Reprimand, Remind, and Retrain. We'll explore why punishment isn't a dirty word; it's the simple, beautiful act of finding out who screwed up and making an example of them so they won't do it again.

So, grab a cup of coffee, sit up straight, and listen up. Safety is as simple as ABC: Always Be Careful. If you can't handle that, then I've got some termination paperwork with your name on it, and I've gotten pretty damn good at filling it out.

The 3 R's™

The Only System You'll Ever Need

Alright, let's get down to business. If you've read the Foreword, you know I'm not here to make friends. I'm here to impart the kind of wisdom that doesn't come from a fancy 'woke' safety conference or some company-mandated webinar. It's the kind of wisdom forged in the crucible of a thirty-five-year career spent sniffing out complacency, praising compliance, punishing failure, and methodically documenting every last detail for the safety trend reports.

Over the years, I've seen safety fads come and go. They all have fancy names, but they always boil down to the same made-up garbage about "systems," "learning," and how "workers are people, too." It's all smoke and mirrors.

What are they really up to?

Well, it's an attack on traditional safety values, plain and simple. They're attempting to tear down our ways of doing things—fear, write-ups, firings—and replace it all with 'learning,' 'improving,' and 'treating workers like people.' It makes me sick to my stomach, y'all.

And for what? I'll tell you for what. These new-age folks with their fancy ideas genuinely hate us and our traditional ways. Make no mistake, this is a safety culture war. Hell, some of them don't even want us saying 'safety culture' anymore! First, they come for our words, then what's next? Our write-ups? Our stand-downs? Soon they'll be replacing first-aid stations with healing crystals. It's an agenda, and they want to soften safety from the inside out.

And the other reason? To sell stuff. Now look, a traditional safety consultant selling their services, books, and procedure templates—that's just good business in my book. But when these other people sell something, well, that's just a snake-oil money grab. They want to sell their services and their books to soft managers who are too afraid to do their actual jobs.

What is a manager's job, you ask? It's to manage. To tell people what to do and make sure they do it. When it comes to safety, it's even simpler: enforce the rules.

That's it. That's the whole game.

And to enforce the rules, you don't need any of that fancy "learning." You need a system that's clear, direct, and effective. A system any simple worker can understand and, more importantly, a system they can fear.

That's why, about twenty years ago, after witnessing a particularly creative deficit of situational awareness involving a forklift and a bollard, I perfected the system that has become my legacy. It's the cornerstone of every safety award sitting in my office. I call it The 3 R's™, and I've trademarked it, so don't even think about putting it on a coffee mug or even talking about it without cutting me a check. If you read that out loud, you owe me $12.95. I accept cash, checks, money orders, and all major credit cards (excluding American Express).

The ***3 R's™*** are:

R*eprimand*
R*emind*
R*etrain*

That's it. It's a beautiful, elegant system of pure, unadulterated accountability. It's the engine of a safe workplace. Every other safety program is just a fluffy, feel-good distraction. This is the real deal. This is how you get results. So, shut your mouth, open your ears, and let's break it down.

The First R: Reprimand *– The Joy of Accountability*

Let's start with my favorite part of the day. The reprimand.

The modern safety guru will tell you that punishment doesn't work. They'll say it creates a culture of fear and drives reporting underground.

I say, good.

If reporting goes underground, who cares? I don't need you to report anything. I've got eyes everywhere: cameras, informants, leaders doing safety observations. If you cause an incident, someone will see it. And they will tell me—because if they don't, I'll fire them right along with you.

You see, my job is to find your mistakes. And when I do, I make damn sure that you, and everyone watching, understand that mistakes have consequences.

A reprimand is not a "coaching moment." It's not a "conversation." It is a verbal slap in the mouth that says, "You have failed."

It's the essential first step in correcting bad behavior. Without the reprimand, there is no accountability. And without accountability, you have chaos. You have workers thinking they can make up their own rules or, worse, that they know better than the company, their leader, or even the safety man.

You have anarchy!

But a truly effective reprimand is an art form. You can't just yell. Any fool can yell. A Darrell-level reprimand is about posture, tone, and paperwork.

The Setting: First, you must choose your location. Never, ever reprimand someone in private. That's a rookie mistake. A private reprimand is a wasted opportunity. The goal is not just to correct one worker; it's to educate the entire herd. The reprimand should take place on the spot, right where the infraction occurred. If a guy isn't wearing his safety glasses, you stop him at the grinder. You want his coworkers to stop what they're doing. You want them to watch. You want them to think, "Better him than me." It's the most effective deterrent known to man.

The Stance: Your body language is crucial. I call it the "Clipboard Power Stance." You approach the offender with purpose. Walk briskly. Plant your feet shoulder-width apart, about two feet from them. This invades their personal space just enough to make them uncomfortable. Puff out your chest slightly. Square your shoulders. Hold your clipboard firmly in one hand, with the pen poised in the other. The clipboard is your scepter of authority. It says, "I am official. I am documenting your failure. This is going in your file."

The Opening Salvo: Do not start with "Can I talk to you for a second?" That's weak. You are not asking for permission. Safety needs no permission. You start with a sharp, loud declaration of their name. "BOB!" Let it echo. Let the silence that follows hang in the air for a second or two. Let Bob's blood run cold.

Then, you state the infraction in the simplest terms. "Bob! Safety glasses. Where are they?" Don't ask why he's not wearing them. His reason is irrelevant. It's an excuse, and there are no excuses for unsafety—ever. He might say they're foggy. He might say they're in his locker. He might say they pinch his nose. I don't care if Christ Almighty himself swooped down and plucked them off his face. The rule is the rule.

The Lecture: This is where you drive the point home. You use simple, powerful, and condescending questions.

"Did you forget the rules this morning, Bob?"

"Is there a part of 'Safety Glasses Required In This Area' that you don't understand?"

"Do you have a spare set of eyeballs at home, Bob?"

I had a guy once—we'll call him Carl—who told me the safety guard on his grinder was slowing him down. I stopped the entire job site. I got up on a stack of pallets (after donning fall arrest protection, of course) and delivered a 45-minute speech about Carl's desire to trade five seconds of production time for a lifetime of learning how to tie his shoes with one hand. Was it humiliating for Carl? You bet it was. That's the whole point! Because did anyone on that site ever remove a safety guard again? Absolutely not. I never got another report or even heard the first peep about people ever removing guards again from that day forward. That, my friends, is effective management.

The Paperwork: The finale of the reprimand is the write-up. As you're lecturing, you should be making notes on your clipboard. Scratch the pen aggressively. Let them hear it. It's the sound of their employment inching towards an early end. Then, you have them sign it. They'll often say, "Signing this admits guilt." My response is always the same: "You're already guilty. Signing this just proves you listened to me."

The reprimand is the shock to the system. It's the cold, hard slap of reality. It establishes the foundation of the 3 R's™ by making one thing crystal clear: there is a right way, a wrong way, and Darrell's way. And Darrell's way is the only one that doesn't end with a write-up.

***The Second R: Remind** – Constant, Annoying, and Necessary*

So, you've reprimanded Carl. He's been shamed, lectured, and written up. Is the problem solved? Of course not. Because the average worker doesn't have the same memory as us safety professionals or leaders. They'll be back to their old, unsafe habits by lunchtime.

That's where the second, and perhaps most tedious, R comes in: Remind.

If the reprimand is a lightning strike, the reminder is acid rain. It's a constant, pervasive, and slightly irritating presence that never lets them forget the rules. This is how you really build what we award-winning safety professionals call a "safety culture." Think of it as "strategic and constant safety nagging." These workers really need it.

Your goal as a safety leader is to become the little voice in their head that's always whispering, "Safety is always watching."

But don't save reminding for after a worker messes up. Start reminding now. About everything safety-related.

Signage, Signage, and More Signage: Your workplace should be absolutely plastered with safety signs. I'm not talking about a few tasteful, professionally printed signs. Nope. Every wall, every machine, every doorway should have a sign. And they shouldn't be polite. None of this "Please Watch Your Step" nonsense. I want signs that yell.

- USE ALL CAPS. It's the visual equivalent of shouting.
- Use bright, obnoxious colors. Yellow, red, orange. Colors that hurt the eyes.
- Use simple, threatening language. "DANGER: THIS MACHINE HAS NO BRAIN. USE YOURS." Or "WARNING: DO NOT ENTER. SEVERE INJURY OR DEATH WILL OCCUR."

Pictures are good. Not of people smiling and wearing PPE. I want pictures of injuries. A little gore is a great motivator. I once put up a poster of a degloved hand next to a conveyor belt. Sure, a lot of people complained. One even threw up. I call that a success. It was a small price to pay to let these workers know that injuries are very, very real.

If you think you have enough signs, you're wrong. Double it. I want your workers to see safety warnings in their dreams.

The Morning Monologue: Every day should start with a safety reminder. Not a conversation. A monologue. Delivered by a safety man. Gather the troops for 20 minutes before their shift starts. Pick a rule from the book—any rule—and have the safety man read it to them. It doesn't have to be relevant to their work that day. One day, read the section on ladder safety. The next, read the policy on handling hazardous chemicals, even if you're in a woodworking shop. The point is not the content; it's the ritual. It's the daily reminder that there is a book of rules, and I, Darrell, have read it, and I expect you to live by it.

The Power of Presence: You need to be seen. You need to walk the floor constantly. Don't smile. Don't engage in chit-chat. Just walk, and watch. Your presence is a reminder. I developed a technique I call the "Safety Stare-Down." If I see a worker from across the floor, I'll just stop and stare at them. I won't move. I'll just lock my eyes on them. Nine times out of ten, they'll get nervous. They'll start checking their PPE. They'll look around to see what they might be doing wrong. They'll correct a behavior they haven't even performed yet. I haven't said a word, and yet I've heroically prevented a potentially tragic incident. It's brilliantly effective and efficient.

Weaponize Catchphrases: You need a handful of simple, repeatable phrases that you can bark at a moment's notice. These are your verbal reminders. They should be short, punchy, and impossible to misinterpret.

"Get your mind on task!"

"Stay aware, stay alive!"

"Don't become a statistic!"

"Safety is no accident!"

Yell them across the shop floor. Say them as you walk past a workstation. It doesn't matter if they're doing anything wrong. It's a constant tune-up, keeping the engine of compliance humming. The reminder phase is a war of attrition. You are trying to wear down their natural tendency towards unsafety, carelessness, laziness, and stupidity. You will never win the war, but you can win the daily battles through sheer, unrelenting persistence.

The Third R: Retrain – *If at First You Don't Succeed, Train, Train, Train Again*

You've reprimanded them. You've reminded them. And yet, some of them still don't get it. You'll catch Carl, for the third time in a week, using a screwdriver as a pry bar or beating away at something with a "wrench hammer." This is when you must deploy the third and final R: Retrain.

Let me be clear. "Retraining" is not about skill development. It's not an opportunity for growth. It is a punishment disguised as education. It's a formal process designed to be so tedious, so patronizing, and so mind-numbingly boring that the employee will do anything to avoid ever having to go through it again.

The Chamber of Learning: The retraining session must take place in your office. It should be small, windowless, and uncomfortable. The walls should be decorated with those gruesome injury posters I mentioned earlier. The employee should sit in a wobbly chair while you sit behind your large, imposing desk. On the desk should be a single object: the tool or piece of equipment they misused.

The Process: Let's use Carl and his screwdriver. The retraining would go something like this.
First, you let him sit in silence for five minutes. Let the awkwardness marinate. Then, you begin.

"Carl," you say, without looking up from your paperwork. "We're here because you seem to have forgotten the purpose of this." You slide the screwdriver across the desk. “Tell me, Carl. What is this?”

He’ll say, “It’s a screwdriver.”

“Correct. Ten points,” you’ll say, with maximum sarcasm. “And what, Carl, does a screwdriver do?”

He’ll say it drives screws.

“It drives screws,” you repeat, slowly, as if talking to a child. “Now, what did you use it for, Carl?”

He’ll mumble something about prying something open.

This is where the magic happens. You stand up. You pick up the screwdriver. You hold it in front of his face. “Carl, I’m going to teach you something. This is a screwdriver. It is for screws. This is a pry bar. It is for prying.” You hold up a pry bar. “They are not the same. Can you say that for me, Carl?”

You make him repeat it. “The screwdriver is for screws. The pry bar is for prying.” You make him say it ten times. Then you move on to the practical portion.

The Lab: You take Carl out to the floor. You have a box of screws and a block of wood. You make him drive screws into the wood for thirty minutes. You watch him. You correct his grip. You critique his form. You make the process as painfully dull as possible. If he used a ladder incorrectly, you make him set up and take down a ladder for an hour. If he didn't use the lock-out tag-out procedure correctly, you make him practice locking and unlocking a breaker box until his fingers bleed.

The point is not to teach him how to use a screwdriver. He already knows. The point is to associate the misuse of that tool with a profoundly unpleasant memory.

The Graduation Ceremony: The retraining concludes back in your office. You present him with a document. It says, "I, Carl, have been retrained on the proper use of a screwdriver. I understand that it is to be used for driving screws and not for prying. I understand that any further misuse will result in further disciplinary action, up to and including termination."

You make him read it aloud. Then you make him sign it. You file it away in his permanent record. You shake his hand limply and say, "Don't let me see you in here again, Carl."

The 3 R's™ is a perfect system. It begins with the public shame of the Reprimand, transitions into the constant nagging of the Reminder, and culminates in the soul-crushing boredom of the Retrain. It's a cradle-to-grave compliance strategy. It addresses the worker not as a partner, but as what they are: a problem. A problem to be managed.

Master this system, and you will have mastered the art of old-school safety. You won't win any awards for empathy, but you'll have a compliant workforce and a pristine incident log. And at the end of the day, that's the only thing that really matters.

Now, let's talk about what it means to be a real leader.

Leaders Are Smarter

That's Why They're in Charge

So, you've mastered The ***3 R's™***. You've tasted the sweet satisfaction of a well-executed public reprimand. You've wallpapered your facility with so much signage that you're on the local print shop's Christmas card list. You've made a grown man practice using a screwdriver for thirty agonizing minutes. Congratulations. You've taken your first step backward into the good ol' days of Safety.

But a system such as The ***3 R's™***, no matter how perfect, is just a tool. A hammer doesn't build a house on its own. It needs a firm hand to swing it. The ***3 R's™*** need a leader to execute them with the proper mixture of authority and barely concealed contempt. And that, my friend, is where most companies fail. They put the wrong people in charge.

In the last twenty years, the whole idea of "leadership" has been hijacked by a bunch of hippies who wouldn't know a real leader if one walked up and handed them a write-up. They sell books talking about caring more, listening better, and being vulnerable. They host seminars where they have you do "trust falls" and talk about your "why." It's an entire industry of engineered propaganda designed to make strong leaders weak and weak leaders feel like they're in charge.

Let me tell you what leadership really is. It's not about serving. It's not about being vulnerable. It's about being smarter than everyone else in the room and having the guts to act like it.

Leaders are the responsible grown-ups. Workers are the children. Some are well-behaved and get pizza parties and ice cream. Some are uncaring little brats and get the time-out corner.

It's about understanding the natural order of things. In any group of animals, there's a leader. The lion doesn't get elected. He's the lion because he's the lion. The rest are sheep or hyenas or whatever other critter knows its place. The workplace is no different. It's an industrial jungle, and the person with the corner office and the reserved parking spot—or the guy with a safety trailer and a golf cart, like yours truly—is the ruler of it. End of story.

If you were meant to be a leader, you'd be one. If you're reading this book because you are a leader, then it's time to start acting like it. It's time to shed the ridiculous notion that you're just "one of the team." You are not one of the team. You are special. You are smarter. You are, in fact, a better person than your workers. You try harder and care more than they do.

You have more skin in the game. If they get hurt, no matter how bad, it always hurts you worse. Their physical pain is no match for the emotional trauma you suffer having to report THEIR event on the quarterly safety call, as if it were your own. You're the parent, the coach, the general, and the warden all rolled into one. Your job is not to be liked; it's to be obeyed.

So, pull up your big-leader pants and let's talk about what it means to be a real leader. A Darrell-level leader.

The single most important thing a leader must understand is the sanctity of the chain of command. The organizational chart is not just a bunch of boxes and lines; it is sacred. It is a map of intelligence, of care, of skill. The people at the top are at the top because they have the biggest brains. They care the most. They know best how work should be done. The people at the bottom are at the bottom because their primary function is to turn a wrench or push a broom without having an injury. That's it. No thinking required. They care the least. They have the least amount of understanding about how work should be done.

Your job as a leader is to defend this hierarchy at all costs. Any attempt by a subordinate to question a decision, offer an unsolicited opinion, ask a question, or—God forbid—challenge your authority must be crushed swiftly and mercilessly.

I was once in a meeting where a young, hotshot engineer tried to tell me that one of my safety plans was "sub-optimal." He had a PowerPoint presentation—which I usually love—trying to poke holes in my old-school, tried-and-true safety strategies. It was adorable.

I let him talk for about three minutes. I listened to him prattle on about involving employees in writing the plan, about how eighteen observation cards per employee per day was unrealistic, about how "trying harder to be more safe" wasn't a real safety strategy. Then, I held up my hand.

The room fell silent. I looked him dead in the eye and said, "Son, how many safety awards have you won?"

He looked at me, real confused like.

I said, "How many years have you been a safety man?"

He stammered. He said that wasn't the point. What did that matter?

"That," I said, leaning forward, "is the only point. I have 35 years as a safety man and three awards. You have zero years of experience as a safety man and zero awards. That means my plan is at least 38 times better than yours. Meeting adjourned."

I didn't even look at his PowerPoint. Why would I? To my highly seasoned and award-winning safety eyes, it was the intellectual equivalent of a child's crayon drawing. It was a nice effort, but it belonged on a refrigerator, not in a serious discussion about safety.

You see, the moment you entertain the idea that a subordinate might have a better idea than you, you have lost. You have introduced doubt into the system. You have told the sheep that they can question the shepherd. You have let the inmates think they are on the same level as the warden. And once that happens, it's only a matter of time before the whole company goes belly up.

A leader's authority must be absolute. It must be unquestioned. Your decisions are not the start of a conversation; they are the final word. The rank-and-file are not paid to think; they are paid to do. Your job is to do the thinking for them. It's a heavy burden, but that's why you get the bigger paycheck—it's for your bigger brain.

Command, Don't Collaborate

The modern workplace is obsessed with "collaboration." They want brainstorming sessions and focus groups and team-building exercises. It's all a colossal waste of time. Collaboration is what happens when a leader is too scared to make a decision.

A true leader does not collaborate. A true leader commands. Your primary tools are not whiteboards and sticky notes; they are directives and deadlines.

The Suggestion Box of Sorrows: If you have a suggestion box in your workplace, I want you to take it off the wall right now. Take it outside, douse it in lighter fluid, and set it on fire (after securing a properly completed hot work permit approved by your local safety professional, of course). The suggestion box is the single worst invention in the history of management. It is an open invitation for every malcontent and armchair expert in your facility to share their half-baked ideas and petty grievances.

What do you get from a suggestion box? You get anonymous notes complaining about the quality of the toilet paper. You get passive-aggressive comments about how the safety man sits in his office and watches YouTube all day. You get a hundred terrible ideas for every one that is merely mediocre.

I had a guy—we'll call him "Ideas Dan"—who put a suggestion in the box every single day. He wanted to rearrange the tool crib. He wanted to change the brand of coffee. He wanted to paint the forklifts orange for "better visibility." Always talking about how this equipment is unsafe or how that thing could kill someone. What does Dan know? Nothing. He's not a Safety Professional. He's not even a leader.

Now, I didn't fire Dan for his stupidity, although I could have. Nope. I had a better idea—the kind of idea workers never think of. I didn't fire him; I promoted him. I made him the "Director of Suggestion Box Analysis." His only job was to read every suggestion, copy them by hand in triplicate, and then file them in the shredder. He quit in a month. Problem solved.

If you want to know how to improve a process, don't ask the person doing it. They're too close to the problem. They can't see the big picture. You, the leader, are the only one with the proper vantage point. You stand on the mountain of leadership while they are lost in the weeds of work. Your job is to tell them which way to go, what to do, how to do it—and to do it the way you said, no excuses or else.

The Art of the Leader Safety Talk:

Meetings are the enemy of productivity. Most meetings are just a collection of people sitting in a room, trying to look busy while they think about what they're going to have for lunch. A leader should avoid meetings whenever possible. Unless they are safety meetings.

While your best bet is to have a seasoned safety professional run your safety meetings for you, a leader should occasionally have what I call a "Leader Safety Talk." Think of it as similar to the Morning Monologue we discussed last chapter. It's a one-way communication designed to disseminate safety information and issue orders.

Here are the rules for a successful Leader Safety Talk:

- Keep it short. No more than ten minutes. Remember, workers' brains don't work quite like our superior leadership brains. Their attention spans are short.

- No chairs. Everyone stands. Standing creates a sense of urgency and keeps them on edge.

- You are the only one who talks. This is not a debate. It is a broadcast.

- End with a clear directive. "Alright, you have your orders. Get to work."

What if someone tries to ask a question? You shut it down. You use one of my patented "Question Killer" phrases:

- *"That's above your pay grade."*
- *"We've already thought of that."*
- *"Just do it the way I told you."*
- *"Are you questioning my leadership?"* (This is the nuclear option. Use it wisely.)

Your communication should be clear, concise, and final. It should flow in one direction: from your brain to their hands.

<u>The Leader on the Prowl: Projecting Infallibility</u>

How you carry yourself on the floor is just as important as the orders you give. You are a symbol. You are a walking, talking embodiment of the rules. You must project an aura of unshakable confidence and borderline omniscience.

These fancy new safety people and leadership consultants will tell you to be approachable, to be curious, to ask good questions and learn from the workers you speak to. This is terrible advice. You are not there to be curious, to learn, or to ask questions. You are certainly not their friend. You are a leader, for goodness' sake. You are their superior. All of that learning and curiosity stuff? That being personable and approachable stuff? It's weakness on full display.

Instead, you must practice what I call "The Leadership Prowl." It's a specific way of walking the floor designed to maximize intimidation and reinforce your authority.

The Mechanics of the Prowl:

- The Pace: Your pace should be brisk and purposeful, but not rushed. You are a shark gliding through the water. You are not a minnow, darting about nervously.

- The Path: Never walk the same path twice. Be unpredictable. They should never know when or where you will appear. They should feel a constant, low-grade anxiety that at any moment, Darrell could materialize behind them.

- The Gaze: Your eyes should always be scanning. Look at the machines. Look at the floor. Look at the ceiling. And most importantly, look at the workers. But don't make eye contact for too long. A quick, piercing glance is all you need. It says, “I see you. I see everything.” Keep an expression of angry confusion on your face at all times to get the most bang for your buck.

Advanced Prowling Techniques:

- The Point and Scowl: If you see something you don’t like, you don’t need to say anything. Just stop, point at the offending object or person, and scowl. Hold the scowl for three to five seconds. Then, shake your head in disappointment and walk away. The worker will spend the rest of the day trying to figure out what they did wrong. It’s a magnificent form of psychological warfare.

- The Strategic Silence: Stand in a high-traffic area and just watch. Don’t say anything. Don’t do anything. Just stand there, with your arms crossed, observing. The silence will become deafening. The productivity of everyone in your line of sight will increase by at least 15%. They will assume you are there because of a problem, and they will work harder to prove they are not the problem.

- The Phantom Note: While observing a worker, pull out your clipboard and jot down a note. Make sure they see you do it. The note can be your grocery list for all it matters. The worker will assume you are documenting an infraction. It's a pre-emptive reprimand.

Your physical presence is a weapon. Use it. You are not there to build relationships. You are there to build compliance.

The Leader's Mind: The Gut and The Rulebook

How does a true leader make decisions? It's simple. You have two sources of truth: The Rulebook and The Gut.

The Rulebook is your bible. It contains the collected wisdom of the company. It has a procedure for everything. If a situation arises, your first question should be, "What does the book say?" If the book has a clear answer, then that is the answer. There is no room for interpretation or debate. The rule is the rule.

But what about situations that aren't in the book? What about those messy, unpredictable moments that require a judgment call? That's where The Gut comes in.

A leader's gut is a finely tuned instrument. It's a supercomputer that processes years of experience, wisdom, and innate superiority into a single, perfect decision. You must learn to trust your gut above all else. Trust it more than data. Trust it more than experts. Trust it more than the pleas of your subordinates. Your gut is never wrong.

I once had a situation where a new piece of equipment was malfunctioning. The engineers were stumped. They had spreadsheets and diagnostic reports and a conference call with the manufacturer in Germany. They were talking about circuit boards and hydraulic pressure and software glitches. They were getting nowhere.
I walked over, took one look at the machine, and said, "Kick it."

The lead engineer looked at me like I had two heads. He said, "Kick it? Darrell, this is a half-million-dollar piece of German engineering. We can't just kick it."

"The book doesn't say you can't kick it," I replied. "My gut says kick it. So, kick it. Right there, on the access panel."

He refused. So, I did it myself. I gave the panel a good, solid whack with my steel-toed boot. The machine sputtered, whirred, and then hummed to life. It worked perfectly.

The engineers were speechless. They couldn't explain it. Of course, they couldn't. They were trying to use logic. I was using a higher form of reasoning: The Gut. I didn't know why it would work. I just knew it would. That's leadership.

When you make a decision, state it with absolute conviction. Never show doubt. Never say, "I think we should..." Say, "Here is what we are going to do." If someone asks you to explain your reasoning, just say, "My gut tells me this is the right way." There's no arguing with that. It's the ultimate trump card.

And if your gut decision turns out to be wrong? That's impossible. If a gut decision leads to a bad outcome, it's not because the decision was wrong. It's because the execution was flawed. Which brings us to the most important skill in a leader's arsenal: blame.

A leader is accountable for everything but blamed for nothing. When things go well, you take the credit. Your brilliant strategy and unwavering leadership led to success. When things go poorly, it is always, always someone else's fault. A worker failed to follow a simple instruction. A supervisor didn't enforce the standard. The team lacked the care to execute your perfect plan.

Your job is to find the point of failure, and that point is always as far down the chain of command as possible. You must become a master of deflecting. It's not about passing the buck; it's about ensuring the buck stops where it belongs: with the person who actually messed up.

Master these principles, and you will be more than a manager. You will be a true leader. Even better, you will be a safety leader. A good ol' fashioned safety leader!

Your employees won't like you. They won't admire you. They won't respect you. But they will fear and obey you.

Safety is as Simple as ABC

Always Be Careful

Alright, let's have a little heart-to-heart. We've covered my battle-tested 3 R's™ system. We've established the natural law of the workplace: that leaders lead because their brains are bigger. If you've been paying attention—and for your sake, I hope you have—you should be starting to see the beautiful, simple architecture of a well-run, safe facility taking shape in your mind. It's a sturdy, no-nonsense structure built on the bedrock of authority and discipline.

But now we must address the rot. We have to talk about the termites that have been chewing away at the foundation of common sense for the last thirty years. I'm talking about the cult of complexity.

Sometime around when they started letting everyone have a trophy just for showing up, a new breed of safety "professional" emerged. They invented a whole new language, a gobbledygook of acronyms and buzzwords designed to make the simple act of not getting hurt sound like rocket science. They talked about "complexity," "human and organizational performance," "psychosocial hazards," and "systems thinking." They drew complicated diagrams that looked like a plate of blue spaghetti fell on a wiring schematic, all in an effort to explain the painfully obvious. They created a fog that only confused our simple-minded workers and drew their attention away from what they should be focusing on—being more careful!

In this mumbo jumbo, they claim that accidents are complex.

Let me tell you the truth. The truth is so simple, so pure, and so powerful. The truth is that accidents are not complex. The machines are not complex. The rules are not complex. The world is not complex. The only variable, the only weak point, the only thing that ever truly breaks down is the worker.

Safety isn't about understanding how thing happen. It's about managing stupidity. It's about being safe, paying attention, and never, ever losing situational awareness. It's about keeping your head on a swivel, following the rules, and being your brother's keeper—or I'll fire you. It all boils down to a simple three-word mantra, a philosophy so powerful it can cut through any "complexity" (if that's even a real word). It is the beginning, the middle, and the end of all true safety. I call it the ABCs.

Always Be Careful.

That's it. That's the whole secret. Write it down. Tattoo it on your arm if you have to. Everything else—every rule, every procedure, every guardrail—is just a footnote to this fundamental law. If every worker, in every moment, simply followed this one, elegant principle, my job would be obsolete. I could finally retire to my cabin fulltime and spend my days fishing, writing my memoirs, reading OSHA regulations, and reflecting on a career spent winning the war against human behavior.

When things go wrong, when people get hurt, when tragedy strikes, it's because they weren't following the ABCs. This new-fangled approach completely misses the point that bad workers cause accidents. They get buried in trying to learn and improve and miss the obvious answer that's sitting right there on the surface: Bad worker!

In the good ol' days, when an incident happened, we had a simple goal: find out who messed up and make sure they never did it again. But somewhere along the line, the world of incident investigation got hijacked. It's no longer about finding fault; it's a treasure hunt for excuses.

They've invented all sorts of fancy techniques for this. Let's look at one of their favorites, the "Five Whys," a tool practically designed to let the guilty party off the hook.

The modern "expert" starts his investigation:

1. **Why** did Johnson slice his finger? *Because he wasn't wearing his cut-resistant gloves.*
2. **Why** wasn't he wearing his gloves? *Because they weren't available in the tool room.*
3. **Why** were they not available in the tool room? *Because the company eliminated that specific PPE item due to budget cuts.*
4. **Why** were essential safety items cut from the budget? *Because the company made a conscious decision to prioritize short-term cost savings over the known and documented risk of employee injury.*
5. **Why** would the company make that decision? *Because our current business culture treats employee safety as a line-item expense to be managed, not a core value to be protected at all costs.*

See their game? In five simple steps, they've blamed Johnson's boo-boo on the CEO. It's a masterpiece of cowardly blame-shifting, and it's flat-out wrong.

Now, here's the Darrell "One Why" method. It's faster, more accurate, and doesn't require a pot of stale coffee.

An incident occurs: Johnson sliced his finger on a piece of sheet metal.

1. **Why** did Johnson slice his finger? *Because he wasn't paying attention.*

End of investigation. Simple. Effective. True.

But believe it or not, the "Five Whys" isn't even the worst of it. Lately, a new plague has descended upon the safety world. They call them "Learning Teams."

These safety nut jobs will tell you that a "learning team" is a way to learn from those nearest to the work about how work actually happens so we can improve together. You know what I call that? Just plain stupid.

You know how work happens? I sure do. It happens the way it says in the procedure. And if it's not happening that way, that's not a learning opportunity, that's a firing.

Let me translate this woo-woo garbage for you. It's a therapy session disguised as an investigation.

One of the rules of a "learning team" says that it should not look for blame. So, what do these new safety people do with their fancy learning teams? They include the person who caused the event to learn from their perspective.

Can you believe the nerve? That's like asking a murderer to sit on the jury at his own trial. "Well, Mr. Killer, what did we learn from this unfortunate stabbing? Any ideas for improving our knife-control policies?" It's a complete abdication of responsibility.

Their whole philosophy is built on the idea that "workers have the best knowledge of how work gets done." That's a joke. Workers have the best knowledge of the break schedule and what's for lunch. They say "people are the solution." No. People are the variable you need to control—forcefully.

When safety events happen, you need a real investigation, conducted by a seasoned safety man like me who isn't afraid to find out who screwed up. The only "learning" that needs to happen is the lesson that mistakes have consequences. And I'm the best teacher they'll ever have.

What about the gloves? What about the supervisor? What about the paperwork? Wah, wah, boo-hoo, competing goals, time pressure, lack of support, blah, blah, blah. Shut up. Irrelevant. All of it. The real cause is, and always will be, the same. The worker's mind was not on the task. He was not being careful.

I was once called in to consult on a major incident at a bottling plant. A conveyor line had jammed, and a mechanic, a guy named Frank, had reached in to clear the jam without locking out the machine. The line kicked on, and Frank's arm was mangled. It was a terrible, expensive, and completely avoidable incident.

When I arrived, the place was a circus. There were suits from corporate, engineers from the manufacturer, and a team of "incident investigators" who looked like they'd never seen a piece of machinery up close. They had cordoned off the area like it was a crime scene. They were taking pictures and measurements. They had a fishbone diagram on an easel that was so complicated it looked like the skeleton of a prehistoric monster. They had identified dozens of "contributing factors." They were building a case that the universe had conspired to injure this man.

I listened to this nonsense for an hour. Finally, I couldn't take it anymore. I walked over to the easel, picked up a marker, and drew a big circle around the box at the very end of the fishbone, the one that said, "Frank's arm was injured." I then drew one single line from that box to a new box I drew in the middle of the whiteboard. Inside the new box, I wrote in big, block letters: "FRANK IS AN IDIOT."

The room went silent.

I turned to the room and said, "I don't need no fancy learning to know that a man who sticks his hand in a machine that's still powered on is an idiot! This event happened for one reason and one reason only: because Frank was not being careful. He was thinking about his fishing trip on Saturday, or what he was going to watch on TV that night. He wasn't thinking about the task. He had a brain-fart. And in our line of work, a brain-fart can cost you an arm."

The real cause is always the worker. And the only tool that can fix that is the relentless, unwavering application of the ABCs.

To really practice these ABC's, you need to maintain 100% situational awareness. Your mind must always be on task.

During your shift, your mind is not your own. It is a piece of equipment, on loan to the company, that is just as critical as any other company property. It is your most important tool. And like any tool, it must be maintained, focused, and used only for its intended purpose: the task at hand.

Unfortunately, the modern worker's brain is a cluttered attic full of useless junk. It's overflowing with distractions, worries, and nonsense that have no place on the shop floor. These are the enemies of attention, and a true safety leader must wage a merciless war against them.

The First Enemy: Your Pathetic Little Life

I'm going to be blunt. Nobody here cares about your problems. I don't care that you had a fight with your spouse. I don't care that your kid is failing algebra. I don't care that your cat has a urinary tract infection. The moment you punch that time clock, your personal life ceases to exist. You are being paid to do a job, not to ruminate on your sad little soap opera.

I had a guy once, a good worker named Dave, who suddenly started making stupid mistakes. Dropping things. Misreading measurements. I pulled him aside. I said, "Dave, what's going on? Your mind isn't on safety."

He confessed that his wife had left him. He was a wreck. He couldn't sleep, couldn't eat, couldn't focus.

Did I send him to counseling? Did I give him a week off to "process his feelings"? Of course not. This isn't a charity. It's a place of business.

I looked him in the eye and said, "Dave, safety is the only family you need. Safety is now your wife."

I continued. "I'm sorry for your loss Dave. That's tough. But from 7 a.m. to 4 p.m., you're not Sad Dave the Divorcee. You're Dave the Lathe Operator. And Dave the Lathe Operator needs to keep his fingers attached to his hands. Your wife has already taken half your stuff. Don't let her take your ability to earn a paycheck, too. Now, I want you to go to that machine, and I want you to think about one thing and one thing only: the smooth, consistent, and predictable rotation of that lathe. It will not leave you. It will not lie to you. It will not take the dog. It will just spin. Focus on the spinning, Dave."

It was the best advice he could have received. He needed to compartmentalize. He needed to understand that for eight hours a day, his brain belonged to the company. Your job as a safety leader is to enforce that rental agreement.

The Second Enemy: The Blabbermouth

The second greatest threat to focus is idle chit-chat. A silent workplace is a safe workplace. When mouths are moving, minds are not working. Workers love to gossip. They'll talk about sports, politics, who's dating whom. Every word they speak is a unit of attention stolen from their task.

I have a zero-tolerance policy for conversation in active work areas. You want to talk? Do it on your break. Do it at lunch. Do it in the parking lot after you've clocked out. On my floor, you communicate for one of two reasons: to give a work-related instruction or to use your Stop Work Authority. That's it.

I once found two guys huddled together, laughing. They were part of a spotter crew for a crane lift. A multi-ton piece of equipment was swinging overhead, and they were telling jokes. I didn't yell. I didn't reprimand them. That would have been too easy.

I walked over to the crane operator and told him to stop. I had the two comedians stand directly under the suspended load. Then I made them tell me the joke.

"What?" one of them said, shaking.

"The joke," I said calmly. "It must have been a real knee-slapper. You were willing to bet your lives on it. So, let's hear it. If I laugh, you can go back to work. If I don't... well, let's just say that load is getting heavy."

They couldn't remember the joke. They just stood there, sweating, staring up at the thing that could have turned them into a grease spot. They never told another joke on my floor again. I had reminded them that the price of a cheap laugh could be their lives.

The Third Enemy: The Cell Phone

Of all the modern inventions that have conspired to destroy the human attention span, none is more potent, more insidious, than the cellular phone. It is a portal to a world of distraction, and it has absolutely no place in a dangerous environment.

Workers will tell you they need it for emergencies. That's a lie. If there's an emergency, someone will find them. They want it so they can look at memes, argue with strangers, and watch videos of people dancing.

My policy on phones is simple: I see it, it's mine.

I have a drawer in my desk. I call it The Phone Prison. If I see a worker so much as glance at a phone on the floor, I confiscate it. It goes into The Phone Prison and stays there until the end of their shift. For a second offense, it stays there for a week. A third offense, and I mail it to their home address.

You must be a tyrant on this issue. You must be unyielding. You are not just fighting for their attention; you are fighting for their lives against an enemy that is designed to be addictive.

So, how do we turn the glorious, simple philosophy of "Always Be Careful" into a practical, daily reality? How do we force it into the minds of those who are naturally inclined to be careless?

It requires a multi-pronged attack. It requires you to control the environment, the tools, and the safety culture.

Hazard Recognition for Dummies

Some of these safety nerds love to talk about "risk assessment." They have complicated matrices with color codes and scoring systems. They'll spend a week analyzing a task to determine if it's a "Level 4" or a "Level 5" risk. It's another scam to make things look complicated.

I have a much simpler system. I call it the "DUH" system.

- **D**angerous?
- **U**npredictable?
- **H**ard?

If you look at something and a little voice in your head says, “Huh, that looks like it could probably kill me,” then it’s **dangerous.**

If it can change from "safe" to "dangerous" quickly and sometimes all by itself, then it’s **unpredictable.**

If you dropped it on your foot, would it hurt? Then it’s **hard.**

If something is Dangerous, Unpredictable, or Hard, you should BE CAREFUL around it. That’s it. All you need is a functioning brain stem.

Your job as a leader is to treat your workers as if they don’t have one. You must make the hazards so painfully, cartoonishly obvious that even a blind man couldn’t miss them. I’m a big fan of painting things. If there’s a trip hazard, don’t just put a sign there. Paint the whole damn thing bright yellow. If there’s a low-hanging pipe, paint it with diagonal black and yellow stripes, like a giant bumblebee. Your facility should look like it was decorated by a hyperactive child who just discovered the safety aisle at the hardware store. Subtlety is your enemy.

Procedures: The Words are Law

A procedure is not a suggestion. It is not a helpful

guide. It is a sacred text carried from upon high—the safety office—to mere mortal workers, to be followed and blessed with everlasting safety. Every step must be followed, in order, every single time. No exceptions. No improvising.

The problem is that workers don't read them. They'll skim it once during training and then forget it exists. You must force them to remember.

I invented a fun little game I like to call "Procedure Pop Quiz." At any random moment, I'll walk up to a worker and ask them to recite a step from a relevant procedure. For example, I'll see a guy getting ready to climb a ladder. I'll stop him and say, "Johnson! Step three of the Ladder Safety procedure. Recite it. Now."

If he gets it right, I'll nod and walk away. He'll be relieved. He'll feel like he just dodged a bullet. His focus will be razor-sharp for the rest of the day.

If he gets it wrong, or if he hesitates, he's failed. And failure has consequences. That's when we take a little trip back to the training room for a one-on-one refresher course. He'll spend his lunch break reading the procedure out loud to me until he has it memorized. I guarantee you, he will never forget it again.

Some people call this micromanagement. I call it excellence.

PPE: Your Second Skin

Personal Protective Equipment is the last line of defense between a worker and a bad day. But it's more than that. It is a physical embodiment of the ABC philosophy. It is a constant, tactile reminder to be careful.

When a worker puts on his hard hat, it should feel like he's putting on a helmet before going into battle. When he puts on his safety glasses, he should feel like a pilot scanning the horizon for threats.

But they get lazy. They'll wear the hard hat tipped back on their head like some kind of cool-guy cowboy. They'll hang their safety glasses on their collar. This is an act of profound disrespect. It's a slap in the face to me and to the very concept of safety.

Your enforcement of PPE rules must be draconian. It must be absolute. There are no excuses.

"It's hot, Darrell." *I don't care. The inside of an ambulance is hot, too.*

"They're fogging up, Darrell." *I don't care. Wipe them off. It's a small price to pay for the gift of sight.*

"It's uncomfortable, Darrell." *I don't care. A prosthetic arm is uncomfortable.*

You must be a hawk. You must scan the floor for these infractions constantly. And when you see one, you must swoop down with righteous fury. A violation of PPE rules is not a minor issue. It is a sign of a broken mind—a worker who has forgotten to be careful. And it is your sacred duty to remind them.

So, there you have it. The grand, unifying theory of safety. It's not about systems. It's not about culture. It's not about empowerment or engagement or any other buzzword the consultants are selling this week.

It's about a simple, three-word command: Always Be Careful.

It's about recognizing that the workplace is not a democracy. It is an authoritarian dictatorship, and you are the dictator. It is your job to impose order on the chaos of human nature. It is your job to force people to be safe, even when they are too stupid or too lazy to be safe on their own.

The next time you're in a meeting and someone starts drawing a flowchart to explain a simple problem, I want you to stand up. I want you to walk to the whiteboard. And I want you to write, in big, bold letters, "ABC."

Then, I want you to turn to the room and say, "This is the only system we need."

They might not understand at first. They might call you old-fashioned. They might call you a dinosaur. Let them. The dinosaurs were big, they were powerful, and they didn't have to sit through a single PowerPoint presentation. Wear the label with pride. Because you, my friend, know the truth. And the truth is simple. Safety is as easy as Always Be Careful.

Accountability

Bad Things Happen to Bad Workers

We need to talk...

Pull up a chair. No, not that one, it wobbles. I've put in a work order for it three times. See? A perfect example of the kind of thing we're going to discuss today. Someone will sit in that chair, it'll collapse, and they'll try to blame the chair. They'll blame the maintenance guy. They'll blame the purchasing department for buying cheap chairs. They'll blame me for not putting up a sign. They will blame everyone and everything but the one simple fact at the heart of the matter: they saw the wobble—or they didn't see it because they didn't do a proper hazard analysis—and they sat down anyway.

I have laid out for you the sacred trilogy of my safety philosophy: the unwavering discipline of The 3 R's™, the natural law of Leadership, and the elegant truth of the ABCs. If you have even a modicum of the common sense you were born with, you should now understand that safety is not complicated. It is a simple matter of following rules set by people who are smarter than you, keeping your mouth shut, and above all else, always being careful.

But now we must venture deeper. We must wade into the murky waters where the modern, soft-bellied safety "experts" dare not tread. We must talk about accountability.

What is accountability? The new-age safety crowd will tell you it's about learning and improving. They'll say you shouldn't punish people for honest mistakes, that people are inherently good and blah, blah, blah, blah...

Bullshit.

Accountability is the culpable responsibility that results in the disciplinary action required to fix a problem.

That's it. It's the engine of a high-performing organization with a world-class safety culture. It's quite literally how we get to zero. People have accidents. We punish them. They have fewer and fewer as we keep punishing them, until we get to zero.

Easy as that.

But beyond that, we have to understand that if an accident happens—if any negative outcome occurs—that is the universe telling us that disciplinary action is required.

Why?

Bad things happen to bad workers.

An accident is not a random event. It is a judgment. It is the universe's way of holding up a mirror to a flawed character. It is the physical manifestation of a weak mind, a distracted soul, and a lazy attitude. The workers who get hurt are the ones who, in one way or another, were asking for it.

Every worker who walks through my door starts the day with a clean slate. In my mind, they have a ledger, an invisible accounting of their focus and character. I call it the Character Ledger. Every action they take, every thought they have, either adds credit to the ledger or racks up a debt.

A "good worker" understands this instinctively. He arrives five minutes early. His uniform is clean. His mind is clear. When he picks up a tool, his entire universe shrinks to that tool and the task at hand. Every bolt he tightens, every box he stacks, every button he pushes is a credit. He is building up a surplus of focus, a shield of good habits that makes him practically invincible. He is a professional. He is here to work safely.

A "bad worker," on the other hand, starts bleeding red ink onto his ledger the moment he clocks in. He shuffles in, hungover, already complaining about the weather. That's a debit. He spends ten minutes gossiping by the coffee machine. Another debit. He pulls out his phone to check the sports scores. A huge debit. He starts a task, but his mind isn't on the machine in front of him; it's on the fight he had with his girlfriend, the bill that's overdue, the vacation he can't afford.

Debit. Debit. Debit.

His Character Ledger is a sea of red. He is running a massive focus deficit. He is walking around the shop floor with a sign over his head that only a man like me can see, and it says, "I AM A LIABILITY."

He is no longer just a worker; he is a sponge, soaking up risk. He is a magnet for misfortune. The laws of physics themselves seem to bend around his carelessness. The pallet that would have fallen harmlessly in the aisle will, through some cosmic alignment, wait until he is standing right under it. The sharp edge of metal that a focused worker would have noticed and avoided will leap out and find his unprotected hand.

The other workers will call it bad luck. The investigators will call it a system failure. I will call it what it is: the bill coming due. The Character Ledger is being balanced, and the price is paid in blood, stitches, and lost-time incidents.

Now we arrive at the heart of the matter. What happens when, despite all your best efforts, an accident occurs? What is the proper response?

The modern approach? Everyone gathers around to talk about their feelings. They treat the injured worker like a victim, a poor soul struck down by a cruel and random fate. Everyone wants to "learn." They offer counseling and coddling. They wring their hands and wonder what the company could have done differently. Boo-freaking-hoo.

This is not only wrong; it is a wasted opportunity.

An accident is a moment of pure, unadulterated clarity. It is a live-fire training exercise. It is a sermon, preached not with words, but with consequences. And you, the leader, are the priest. It is your job to interpret this sermon for the congregation.

When a bad worker gets hurt—and you know they were bad because they got hurt—you should feel a little spark of joy.

Hold on, hear me out. I'm not a monster. I don't delight in human suffering. The joy I'm talking about is not sadistic pleasure. It is the quiet, profound satisfaction of seeing order restored. It is the joy of a teacher whose most difficult student has finally, through dramatic failure, understood the lesson. It is the joy of seeing your theory proven correct in the most visceral way possible.

My theory is that good workers don't get hurt and bad workers do. When one of them gets hurt, it is a validation of my entire worldview. It is a chance to prove to everyone else that I was right all along. Therefore, you must capitalize on the incident. You must turn it into a spectacle of accountability.

As soon as the scene is safe and the injured party has been hauled away, you will gather the entire department. You will march them over to the spot where the incident occurred. Is there still blood on the floor? Good. Let them see it.

You will stand over that spot, and you will deliver the eulogy. Not for the worker, but for his bad habits.

"Look here," you will say, pointing. "This is where Johnson decided that thinking about his weekend was more important than watching where he was going. This is the exact spot where his Character Ledger, which has been in the red for months, was finally balanced. He didn't slip on oil. He slipped on his own inattention. Do not feel sorry for Johnson. Feel sorry for the paperwork I have to fill out. And then, take a good, long look at this spot, and make a promise to yourself that you will never stand here."

It's powerful. It's theatrical. It's terrifying. And it's the most effective safety training they will ever receive.

The discipline for the injured worker must be swift, public, and severe. He has not only violated a safety rule—you know a rule was violated because an injury occurred; events can't happen if you're following the rules—he has embarrassed the company. He has created a mess that you have to clean up. The best way to deal with bad workers who get hurt is to hurt them more. This really makes the lesson stick. Cut off your fingers? Well, let's make sure you're off work without pay for a few weeks to think about just how stupid you were. Broken leg? Fired.

I had a guy who broke his ankle because he was carrying a box that was too big and couldn't see the step in front of him. When he came back to work, still in a cast, I assigned him a new role. His job, for a full month, was to stand by that step. His only task was to say, "Watch your step," to every single person who walked by.

It was dehumanizing and humiliating for him. Good. That was the point. And it was a constant, living reminder to everyone else. They didn't just see a step; they saw a monument to a stupid mistake.

An accident is a gift. It is a rare and valuable opportunity to teach a lesson that no poster or procedure ever could. To waste it on empathy or "learning" is the ultimate act of managerial malpractice.

The message of this chapter is not a popular one. It is a hard truth in a world that loves soft lies. The truth is that there are no victims on the shop floor. There are only volunteers.

Every worker, every day, chooses his own fate. He chooses it when he decides to leave his worries at the door or bring them in with him. He chooses it when he decides to follow the procedure or invent his own. He chooses it when he decides to focus or to let his mind wander.

Your job is to force them to make the right choice. You must be the shepherd for a flock that is constantly trying to wander off a cliff. You must be the stern, unforgiving voice of reason in a world of distraction and incompetence.

Accountability is not a dirty word. It is the engine

of excellence. It is the foundation of a truly safe workplace. It is the understanding that actions have consequences, and the person who suffers the consequence is the one who initiated the action. As it should be.

So, the next time an incident occurs, don't ask how things went wrong... Ask what the worker did wrong. Look at their ledger. You will find, every single time, that the bill was long overdue.

The Choice

Be Safe, or ELSE!

We've been on a journey, you and I. I've dragged you through the mud and muck of the real world of safety—a world of concrete floors, spinning blades, and the limitless potential for human error. If you're still with me, then you are ready for the final lesson. This is the one that matters. This is the culmination of every reprimand I've ever delivered, every rule I've ever enforced, every life I've ever saved from the consequences of its own stupidity.

It all comes down to this.

The choice to be safe.

To understand that choice, you first need to understand how we got here and how we move forward. The only way forward in safety is to go backward.

We must return to the good ol' days. Back to a time when leaders were leaders, safety was safety, and workers knew their place! A time when safety meant a good-old-fashioned safety manual, a pre-job brief, a stand-down, and a write-up.

I know what the modern safety professional will say when they hear that. They'll roll their eyes. They'll call me a dinosaur. They'll sneer and talk about "progress" and "evolution." They are fools. They see the last thirty years as a steady march of enlightenment. I see it for what it is: a long, slow, grinding defeat. A methodical erosion of common sense.

I came up in a different time. A better time. A time when safety was simple because the world was simple. You had a job to do. You had rules to follow. If you did your job and followed the rules, you kept your fingers and you took home a paycheck. If you broke the rules, you got hurt, you got fired, or both. There was no confusion. There was no "gray area." There was only the work, the rules, and the consequences.

The safety man in those days was not a "partner." He was not a "coach." He was the law. He walked the floor with the absolute authority of a hanging judge. His word was final. His presence was a constant reminder that the rules were not suggestions. We didn't have "conversations." We didn't do "analysis." We saw a problem, we pointed at it, and we fixed it with a reprimand and a write-up. And it worked. The fear was real, the respect was earned, and the consequences were immediate.

But then, something changed.

Slowly at first, then all at once, the termites got into the foundation. A new breed of safety "professional" began to emerge. They had ideas. They had a vision for a new kind of safety. A softer, kinder, gentler safety.

And they began to wage a war on the old ways. They began to tear down the fortress of common sense, brick by brick. They told us that our methods were outdated and dehumanizing, that our philosophy was barbaric.

They gave us "behavior-based safety," which was a fancy way of saying, "Let's blame the worker, but pretend we're not"—a concept I actually appreciated and enjoyed. But then they decided even that was too mean.

They told us that fear was a bad thing, that it created a "culture of silence." They told us that discipline was counterproductive, that it drove reporting "underground." They told us that the goal was not compliance, but "engagement."

It was a slow, deliberate campaign of indoctrination. And the leaders, the managers, the executives—they bought it all.

And so, the old ways were dismantled. The old guard was retired or retrained into submission.

The safety man was stripped of his authority. He was told to be a partner, a coach, a facilitator.

We have traded simple clarity for confusing curiosity. We have traded discipline for discussion. We have traded accountability for understanding. We must turn back before it's too late. We must turn from our evil and blasphemous new ways. The end of common sense is nigh! Repent, ye safety sinners! Cast out your psychological safety and embrace the righteous fear of the company, lest ye be cast into the pit of unemployment!

The only way forward is to go back. We must have the courage to say that anything different is wrong. We must return to the simple, brutal, and effective truths that kept our grandfathers alive.

You cannot win a war until you understand your enemy. And make no mistake, we are in a war. It is a culture war for the soul of safety in the workplace. On one side, you have men like me—traditionalists, realists, patriots of common sense. On the other side, you have them. The new safety professionals.

Who are these people? What do they want?

You must understand that they are not like you and me. They do not see the world the way we do. We see a factory floor as a place of production, a simple place that must be controlled with rules and discipline. They see it as an "interesting story" of people adapting and figuring stuff out.

We see a worker as they truly are: childlike, with a simple job to do. They see a worker as a grown-up, with good ideas about how to do their job.

We see an accident as a failure of personal responsibility. They see an accident as a "learning opportunity" to be explored.

As you can clearly see, these people are not just wrong. They are dangerous. Dare I say, evil. They are not our allies. They are the enemy—bad actors with a dangerous agenda.

They come preaching the gospel of human performance, which is just a fancy way of saying, "Humans make mistakes, so let's redesign the entire world to be idiot-proof instead of just firing the idiots." They will tell you that you cannot expect a worker to be perfect, that you must build "robust systems" that can tolerate error. What they are really telling you is to surrender. To accept failure as inevitable. To give up on accountability altogether.

They come to you with their learning teams and their post-incident reviews. They will spend hours with your workers, drawing on whiteboards, trying to understand the "story" of the work. They will identify a dozen "improvement ideas" for the company to complete. And do you know what will be missing from that entire report? The simple, obvious truth: Johnson stuck his hand in the damn machine.

But here is the most damning indictment of all. Here is how you know, for certain, that they are the enemy.

They care more about the workers than they care about safety.

Read that again. Let it sink in. They will talk endlessly about the worker's well-being, their feelings, their stress, their "lived experience." They will advocate for the worker, defend the worker, and include the worker. But in doing so, they sacrifice the one thing that actually keeps the worker safe: me, the safety man! My good old-fashioned, tried-and-proven ways! Rules, compliance, and discipline!

We, the traditionalists, are the ones who truly care. We care enough to tell the worker the hard truth. We care enough to hold them to a high standard. We love them so much that we will hurt them to keep them safe. We care enough to punish them when they fail, because we know that a write-up today is better than a funeral tomorrow. Our methods may seem harsh. They may seem cruel. But they are rooted in a deep and abiding respect for the unforgiving reality of the physical world.

They have chosen the worker. We have chosen the safety program. The two are not the same. That is the central conflict of our time. They are trying to tear down our traditional ways and they must be stopped.

So, how do we fight back? How do we win this safety culture war?

We cannot out-think them. We cannot out-talk them.

We can only win by being better. By being stronger. By holding the line in our own facilities and living our traditional safety values every day —living the right way. And it all begins with understanding where the real battle takes place.

The real battle takes place inside the skull of every single worker. It is a battle for their attention, a battle for their focus, a battle of the will.

So that's where we need to go. We need to get inside their skulls.

For decades, the safety industry has been trying to solve the problem with the wrong tools. They have been trying to engineer a solution, to regulate a solution, to train a solution. They have filled libraries with binders, spent billions on consultants, and wrapped the world in so much red tape that it's a miracle anyone can move at all. And yet, people still get hurt.

Why?

Because they have been looking at it as a problem of the workplace. A problem of machines and procedures and environments. They are wrong. It is not a problem of the workplace. It is a problem of the will.

Safety is not a system you can install. It is not a rule you can memorize. It is not a piece of equipment you can wear. Safety, in its purest, most distilled form, is a choice. It is a conscious, continuous, and deeply personal decision that every worker makes a thousand times a day.

And the choice is this: Be Safe, or Else.

That's it. That's the entire game. There is no middle ground. There is no third option. There is no "trying." There is only the stark, binary, black-and-white reality of that choice. Every other rule, every other chapter in this book, is just commentary on this one, terrible, magnificent truth.

So, for one last time, sit up straight and listen. This is the lesson that will save your life, your limb, and your livelihood.

Look at the words carefully. The phrase is not "Stay Safe." "Staying" is passive. It implies that safety is a static condition, a state of being that can be achieved and then maintained with minimal effort. It suggests that the world around you is fundamentally safe, and you just need to avoid stumbling out of that safety.

I am not telling you to "Stay Safe." I am commanding you to "Be Safe."

"To be" is a verb of action. It is a state of constant creation. It is not a place you arrive at; it is a thing you do. It requires effort, energy, and above all, will. To Be Safe is to be engaged in a permanent, unending war against unsafety. It is to be a soldier on the front lines, every second of your shift.

When you walk onto my shop floor, you are entering a battlefield. In this environment, to be anything less than 100% engaged is an act of suicidal negligence.

To Be Safe means that you are constantly, obsessively, hunting for hidden hazards. It means keeping your head on a swivel.

To Be Safe means that when you pick up a tool, you are not just grabbing a hammer. You are entering into a contract with it. You are consciously acknowledging its purpose, its limitations, and its capacity to cause harm if misused. Your focus narrows until the universe consists of only you, the tool, and the task.

To Be Safe means that your mind is a fortress, and you are the guard at the gate. You are actively repelling the invaders of distraction. The argument with your spouse, the score of the big game, the worry about your car payment—these are enemy combatants, and you must strike them down without mercy. You must achieve a state of pure, clear-headed focus on doing your work safely.

This is not easy. In fact, it is the hardest work you will ever do. It is more demanding than any physical labor. It is the work of forging your own safety, moment by moment, out of the raw material of your own will and attention. Most people are not capable of it. They are too weak, too lazy, too distracted. They want safety to be given to them. They want a world where they can be careless without consequence. They want to "stay safe" without having to "be safe."

Those are the people who get hurt.

This brings us to the second half of the equation. The "Or Else."

When you choose to be careless, you are not just breaking one of my rules. You are making a bet. You are betting that you are faster than the machine, smarter than the laws of physics, and luckier than the thousands of workers who have been maimed before you. You are betting your fingers, your eyes, your limbs, your very life, on the hope that this one time, the "Or Else" will not apply to you.

And for a while, you might win that bet. You might get away with the shortcut. You might survive the moment of inattention. And this is the most dangerous thing that can happen. Because every time you win, you get bolder. You start to believe you are immune. You start to think the rules are for other people. You forget the "Or Else" is always there, waiting patiently for you to make one mistake too many.

My reprimands are just a faint echo of the feedback a spinning lathe can provide. My write-ups are just a pale imitation of the report a coroner might write. I am doing you the favor of giving you the gentle warning before the universe gives you the final, catastrophic one.

When you see me on the floor, you should not see a safety manager. You should see a walking, talking embodiment of the "Or Else." You should see the physical manifestation of the consequence you are trying to avoid. Your fear of me is a healthy, rational response. It is a survival instinct.

So, here we are. At the end of the book, and at the beginning of the rest of your working life. I have given you the tools. I have shown you the truth. I have held up a mirror to your own weakness and given you the simple, brutal choice that will define your future.

You can leave this book behind and go back to the way things were. You can join the enemy. You can continue to treat the rules as suggestions and make bets against the "Or Else," hoping your luck holds out. You can continue to be a soft, weak, distracted liability—a bad worker waiting for a bad thing to happen. That is your right. You can make that choice, and I will gladly terminate your employment, making you available to the industry.

Or, you can make the better choice.

You can choose to Be Safe.

You can choose to join the resistance. You can choose to accept that the responsibility is yours, and yours alone. You can choose to forge your will into a weapon. You can choose to become a professional, a master of your own mind, a guardian of your own body. You can choose to care so damn much about going home in one piece that you will not allow anything in the universe to stop you.

The only thing that can protect you is you. Your caring. Your situational awareness. Your focus. Your discipline. Your will.

The choice is simple. It is the only choice that matters.

Be Safe, or Else.

Mandatory Paperwork

Hold it right there. You didn't really think that was it, did you?

What kind of safety man would I be if I didn't leave you with some paperwork? A lousy one, that's the kind.

In the following pages, you'll find some of my favorite, no-nonsense safety resources. This is for all of you joining us good folks out there, helping take safety back to the way it ought to be —back to the good old days.

Enjoy.

Yours is Safety,

Darrell, Safety Man

VIOLATION

Employee Name: ______________________________

Date of Incompetence: ________________________

Rule Ignored (Cite Manual Page #):____________

Brief Description of Violation:

____

____

____

Employee's Excuse:

____

____

Corrective Action Administered (Select One):

[ ] Stern Verbal Warning (Final)
[ ] Disciplinary Write-Up (Final)
[ ] Mandatory Re-Read of Relevant Manual
[ ] Termination (Effective Immediately)

Signatures:

____

Safety Man

____

Employee (Acknowledges Receipt of Consequence)

ONE WHY™

Instructions: *Save time and paperwork. Stop asking pointless questions and get to the actual root cause in under five seconds.*

1. **Why** *did the incident occur?*
(Check all that apply)

[ ] The worker was not paying attention.
[ ] The worker took a shortcut.
[ ] The worker ignored a clearly posted rule.
[ ] The worker did something stupid.

Analysis Complete.

Root Cause Identified: Worker Error.

Case Closed.

Behavior Observation Card

Instructions: *If you see something, say something. Help us identify liabilities before they end up in a report.*

Observer: ______________________________
Subject Being Judged: ____________________

(Check all that apply)

PHYSICAL BEHAVIORS

[ ] Walking too slowly (Wasting time)
[ ] Walking too quickly (Running from work)
[ ] Standing still (Daydreaming)
[ ] Talking to coworker (Plotting/Gossiping)
[ ] Actually working (For now...)

AT-RISK MENTAL STATES (Inferred):

[ ] Exhibiting unwarranted optimism.
[ ] Failure to respect gravity.
[ ] Looks a little too comfortable.
[ ] Demonstrating a clear lack of common sense.
[ ] Acting faster than their brain works.

Action Taken:

[ ] Gave them "The Look."
[ ] Forwarded to Safety for follow-up.

Declaration of Compliance

Instructions: *This is not a discussion. This is a declaration of what will happen. All participants will read, understand, and sign before any tools are touched.*

Job/Task: ________________________________

SECTION 1: THE PLAN (AS DECREED BY MANAGEMENT)

Here is what you will do. Do not think. Do not deviate.

____

____

____

SECTION 2: THINGS THAT WILL HURT YOU

( ) Spinning Things | ( ) Heavy Things | ( ) Hot Things | ( ) Sharp Things | ( ) High Things

SECTION 3: WORKER ACKNOWLEDGEMENT

By signing below, I attest that I have been told what to do and I possess the basic intelligence required not to injure myself today. I understand that any deviation from the plan or failure to respect the things listed in Section 2 will be considered a willful act of self-harm and grounds for immediate termination. I accept that my role is to comply, not to improvise. My opinions are irrelevant and my suggestions are not welcome.

____

Signature of Compliant Worker

About Darrell the Safety Man

Darrell the Safety Man is a multi-award-winning safety professional, and the last line of defense. For over thirty-five years, he has stood in the trenches of safety, waging a relentless, day-in, day-out war against carelessness, stupidity, and lack of situational awareness.
Fed up with the nonsense of "psychological safety," "learning teams," and other feel-good fads that have infected his profession, Darrell decided it was time to fight back. This book is his manifesto. It is built on the bedrock principles that made safety great: accountability, discipline, and the elegant, brutal truth of his signature systems—The 3 R's™ and the ABCs of safety.

In these pages, you won't find any coddling, hand-holding, or buzzwords. You will find the hard-won wisdom of a man who has seen it all and isn't afraid to tell the truth. When he's not on the shop floor saving workers from themselves, Darrell can be found in a small, undisclosed cabin in Arizona, reading OSHA regulations, and waiting for the day when common sense finally makes a comeback.

Made in the USA
Las Vegas, NV
14 August 2025

26365648R00056